THE LUCAN
MISSION

A Teacher's Book of Prayer

James and Katie Howard

THE LUCAN
MISSION

Email: thelucanmission@gmail.com

First Edition 2017

ISBN: 978-1-9999459-0-9

DEDICATION

To our dear friends Tim and Danica

CONTENTS

FOREWORD

As a minister in the Anglican Church, I spend a lot of time encouraging the congregation that I serve to connect their faith in the Lord Jesus with their "work lives". We live in a culture that seeks to relegate religious belief to the private sphere – to private "opinion" or interest. This encourages Christians to compartmentalise their lives; to be a Christian at home and church but a secular, functional atheist at work. Here is not the place to go into the inconsistency of this worldview, but it is worth noting that Jesus, to whom all knees will eventually bow, does not see it this way.

When it comes to prayer, Jesus instructed us to pray that the Father's kingdom would come and His will be done on *earth* as it is in heaven. He makes no distinction or limit regarding what should be prayed for by his followers. As Christians we know that the establishment of the kingdom of God is good news to all people and for every aspect of our lives, including our work and those with whom we work. When we go into the workplace, then, many of us are conscious that we are Christ's ambassadors (2 Corinthians 5:20), but it is easy to forget that we are also part of 'a royal priesthood' (1 Peter 2:9), and that, like all priests, we have been given the privilege and vocation of interceding

1

between God and those around us. When we think of ourselves in this way, it becomes clear that the focus of our prayers should include our work, the 'concerns of others, and especially of those who cannot protect themselves'.[1]

It is true to our experience that prayer seems to come more easily to some than others, and at times we have all been left unsure of what or how to pray. This need not be an embarrassment; we are in good company, even the disciples asked Jesus what and how to pray! His answer, what we now know as the Lord's Prayer, provided both a model and a guide for our prayer. It can be prayed as a whole, as we do during church services, or each line can be taken as a theme for further, specific prayer.

This book of prayer is intended to help people do just this; model how to pray 'your kingdom come, your will be done, on earth as it is in heaven' (Matthew 6:10) within the education sector. James and Katie deeply believe that prayer is a way for us to glorify, delight in, and encounter our Heavenly Father. Combining Katie's experience as a teacher and James's theological study in Oxford, this practical prayer book is grounded in biblical faith and is a great

---

[1] Bartholomew, Ecumenical Patriarch of Constantinople, *Encountering the Mystery: Understanding Orthodox Christianity Today* (2008, Doubleday, New York), 77.

resource for those of us working with young people, as it helps us to integrate our faith with our work and prayer-life.

A Teacher's Book of Prayer invites you to consider the school in which you work as a place where God can and will make a difference in response to His people's prayer. Like the Lord's prayer, the prayers in this book may be read as set prayers, but I would encourage you to use them as a guide to enrich your personal prayers for the people and educational settings in which God has placed you, remembering that His grace is sufficient in all that we do.

Revd David Hazell

PREFACE

The vocational call to teach brings great joy and great responsibility. Working with young people is an immeasurable privilege and a precious gift from God. At times, however, the pressure of educating young minds can leave us with a despondent heart, and lie heavy upon the soul. In these moments of trial and adversity it is pivotal that we, with serious and intent resolve, turn in prayer to our loving and gracious Father. This collection of prayers has been compiled to equip us in that very task, drawing our hearts and minds ever-closer to God, as we partner with Christ in this magnificent vocation to which we have been called. By reflecting on the myriad braids of life in education, from our students and colleagues to our schools and teaching practices, we hope that these prayers will help you to grow in intimate fellowship with Jesus, as you navigate the educational landscape in which you find yourself.

We all falter and struggle in the daily disciplines of the spiritual life. With this in mind, the following chapters seek to guide, encourage and preserve you, with a pattern of prayer that can be seamlessly integrated into the routines of the day. It is our intention that this pastoral resource will fuel private devotion, sustain corporate worship and ultimately serve as a springboard for further meditation and prayer. Each chapter addresses a different dimension of school life and, as such, you may follow the sequence of prayers chronologically or thematically according to your particular spiritual need.

It is through communion with God in prayer that we are truly reminded of His ever-abiding presence in the cares and occupations of our lives. We pray that this collection will energise your walk with Christ, and deepen your commitment to serving the needs of those placed under your care. May your work as educators ever reflect the glorious riches of the gospel, and its saving power dwell richly in your hearts, that you will know more of God's abundant blessing, both in your interaction with young people and life beyond the classroom.

James and Katie Howard

Chapter One

For our Students

For our Students

Whoever welcomes one of these little children in my name
welcomes me; and whoever welcomes me does not welcome me
but the one who sent me.

Mark 9:37

Heavenly Father,

How wonderful is your design, O Lord, that the cycle of learning and teaching takes place in every minute of every day, and in every corner of your marvellous creation. What a privilege it is to teach such a unique group of students, each of whom have been made in your image and likeness. Thank you for their individuality, their creativity and their innocence. Above all, thank you that you know each of them, and that you loved them even before the foundation of the world. Please help them to be curious and insightful in their learning, and preside over them as they grow in discernment, prudence and judgement. Keep their hearts humble, teachable and obedient and their minds safe in the redeeming love of Christ. In hours of perplexity and need, we pray that they, with an upright heart and kindled devotion, would find peace in your secure, reflective and adoring gaze. Grant me, as their teacher, the wisdom and patience to nurture them well, and prepare them for the challenges that await them in the days, months and years ahead.

In your holy and precious name we pray,

Amen.

Their Learning

If any of you lacks wisdom, you should ask God, who gives
generously to all without finding fault, and it will be given to
you.

James 1:5

Wonderful Counsellor,

Though we are infinitely flawed and lack wisdom, by your over-flowing grace you instruct and enlighten us every day, blessing each and every generation with new knowledge and insight. Thank you for the ability to acquire new skills and expertise, and that you created us to learn. I pray that our students would know the intrinsic joy of learning, and that you would instil in them a hunger for wisdom and a thirst for knowledge. Illuminate and strengthen their minds, and grant them sharpened zeal and inquisitiveness as they approach their studies, that they, with sincerity of heart and strength of purpose, would fulfil the potential to which you have called them. Thank you for the manner in which you patiently and generously teach us, and help us to nurture a greater love of learning in our classrooms, that our students may truly know the blessings of intellectual discovery and growth.

In your all-satisfying name we pray,

Amen.

Their Character

But the fruit of the Spirit is love, joy, peace, forbearance,
kindness, goodness, faithfulness, gentleness and self-control.
Against such things there is no law. Those who belong to Christ
Jesus have crucified the flesh with its passions and desires.

Galatians 5:22-24

Prince of everlasting peace,

Thank you that you have not only shown us the way to live through the obedient life and triumphant death of your perfect son, but that you have also given us your Word and your Spirit that we may bear faithful and expansive witness to the glorious gospel of Christ. Awaken in us a fervent desire to follow in your footsteps, and help us as teachers to demonstrate the fruit of the Spirit to our students. Grant that they may learn joy by seeing our solid joy, and will know something of your immeasurable kindness through our dealings with them. I pray for their personal, moral and spiritual development, that they would mature into adulthood, assured by a lively sense of your healing presence and the sweetness of your underserved and never-failing mercy. Teach them, and us their teachers, your perfect ways, that we might become more like you each day and mirror the sacrificial love that you taught us upon the Cross. Thank you for the ways in which you use our momentary struggles to profoundly shape and refine us into a holy and blameless people. We praise you that your life-giving Spirit causes lasting and inevitable change in us, and that we are not saved by our character or the quality of our life, but by the sanctifying power of your pardoning grace.

In over-flowing thanks we pray,

Amen.

Their Attendance

The Lord bless you and keep you;
The Lord make his face shine on you
and be gracious to you;
the Lord turn his face toward you
and give you peace.

Numbers 6:24-26

Gracious and ever-loving God,

Thank you for each and every one of my students; those who really love school and those who find it a challenging or fearful place. Please help me to encourage those disheartened and anxious in spirt, and make them feel welcome and valued as they enter the classroom. Remind me, loving Father, that it is only through the abundant outpouring of your sovereign grace that our interactions with students can and do make a difference to their lives. Please give students who attend school infrequently the strength and confidence to return to the classroom. May I cultivate a safe and supportive learning environment, and fashion constructive and fruitful relationships with my students' parents and guardians, that they too would feel reassured that our school is a secure and rewarding place to be. Thank you for the passion and perseverance of students who are in attendance every day, come rain or shine, and please help us all to make our school a place where light shines, even in darkness.

In the strong and loving name of Jesus,

Amen.

Their Motivation

Whatever you do, whether in word or deed, do it all in the name of the Lord Jesus, giving thanks to God the Father through him.

Colossians 3:17

Lord of Lords,

Those who abide in your everlasting love are freed by the knowledge that you have accomplished all that was necessary for our salvation. In Jesus, with unshakeable confidence, we can worthily proclaim, "it is finished". We pray that this saving knowledge would spark an excitement about learning, and that you would infuse our hearts with the desire to work conscientiously in your mighty name, with hope-filled thanksgiving for the glorious gifts and talents you have bestowed upon us. There are times when we feel demotivated, and opt for idleness over productivity and efficiency. We are truly sorry for this and recognise that it does not bring you glory nor does it bring perfection to the saving work you have begun in us. Refine and strengthen our will in these moments, and grant us purity of heart and a steady, sustained focus as we approach the tasks that you have set before us. Just as you work in the creation and sustenance of all that we need, help us, most gracious Lord, to better reflect your glorious vision of work to our students. May you plant seeds of curiosity in their hearts that they might resound with joy in their education, and help us to nurture their passions and design learning that inspires them. We also ask, that they would be motivated not only by the prospect of excellent grades or progression to the next stage of their studies, but by an intense longing to serve others, and advance and magnify your holy name.

With unending thanks we pray,

Amen.

Their Exams

But he said to me, "My grace is sufficient for you, for my power is made perfect in weakness". Therefore I will boast all the more gladly about my weaknesses, so that Christ's power may rest on me.

2 Corinthians 12:9

Faithful Lord,

Assessment and examination can cause students unbridled anxiety and fear. Yet you, Lord Jesus, teach us that whatever the outcome, your life-affirming grace is sufficient. Please help us, in both word and deed, to manifest this incredible truth to our students, that they would approach their exams with courage, poise and God-rooted confidence. Mercifully grant that we would prepare them well, giving strength in moments of need and counsel in times of perplexity. May they view their exams as an opportunity to demonstrate and apply all that they have learnt. Help us as teachers to humbly remind them that perseverance in the face of failure and adversity is a virtue. When results come, sovereign Lord, we pray for your peace over all outcomes. We also ask that our students would trust in your great plan for their lives, safe in the knowledge that you are always with us, our stronghold and sure defence in all hardship.

Beholding your infinite glory and absolute power we pray,

Amen.

Their Friendships

My command is this: Love each other as I have loved you.
Greater love has no one than this: to lay down one's life for
one's friends.

John 15:12-13

Almighty and eternal God,

Thank you for the enduring beauty and innocence of childhood friendships, and that school is a wonderful place to interact with people from all walks of life, and experience the cherished intimacy and radiant joy of fellowship. I thank you for the many friendships blossoming in my school this day. However, remind me, loving God, that friendship is not a blessing everyone enjoys at school. I pray therefore for the children in my class who find it difficult to make friends and ask that no-one would feel excluded or ostracised within the school community. Please safeguard their hearts and remind them that with you, they are never alone and that in you, they have the greatest companion they could ever ask for. Grant that they may make friends who encourage and support them, and help them to flourish, not wither. We pray too that the influence of our students upon one another would be positive, that they may build each other up rather than tempt one another to sin. We thank you for the surpassing beauty of friendship, and the loving care that surrounds us on every side, and ultimately, we pray that all would find refuge in the embrace of Jesus, our ultimate and everlasting friend.

With a true heart of faith we pray,

Amen.

Their Futures

"For I know the plans I have for you", declares the LORD, "plans to prosper you and not to harm you, plans to give you hope and a future".

Jeremiah 29:11

Name above all names,

Thank you that you know and have surely set the path for each one of us, including those I have the pleasure of teaching. Thank you that you know each of them intimately and that each one is fearfully and wonderfully made by your upholding hand. You are the author and architect of their futures, and I pray that they would entrust their lives to you. Whatever their vocation, we pray that you would help them to make a concrete and significant difference to the world. Grant them the skills, expertise and knowledge to make a smooth transition from education to employment, and reassure them that while work is important, our ultimate hope and true identity are found in you. In each season of their lives, would they seek your kingdom first, and may they trust that you work through both good and bad experiences to bring about your glorious and redemptive purposes.

Thank you that their futures are safe in your hands,

Amen.

Chapter Two

For our Colleagues

For our Colleagues

For what we preach is not ourselves, but Jesus Christ as Lord, and ourselves as your servants for Jesus' sake. For God, who said, "Let light shine out of darkness", made his light shine in our hearts to give us the light of the knowledge of God's glory displayed in the face of Christ.

2 Corinthians 4:5-6

Christ our everlasting light,

Thank you for the brilliant diversity of staff that make up the fabric of our school; from the catering staff and teaching assistants to administrative staff and caretakers, would each and every member of the team feel equally valued. Thank you that our school is a reflection of the society we serve, and a microcosm of the world you have created. We pray that it would be a stimulating and warm environment for all, in which the grace of charity abounds and a culture of solidarity and harmony prevails. I pray for my colleagues that they may know you, the light of the world, and that in whatever darkness they face, your perpetual light may shine in their hearts. By the might of your Spirit, grant me the wisdom and kindness to be a good colleague to those in my school and help me to seek out and pray for, and with, those who feel lost and forsaken. Grant that I would be committed to providing a living witness to your strong love and victorious salvation.

In Jesus' mighty name we pray,

Amen.

School Governance

Then Jesus came to them and said, "All authority in heaven and on earth has been given to me".

Matthew 28:18

My Strength and my Redeemer,

Thank you for those you have blessed with the skills to lead our schools. May they be unselfish in service, walk humbly and do justly with pure intention. Help us to respect those for whom we work and those who work for us in equal measure. Grant us the courage and resolve to considerately and calmly challenge any decisions that we feel would do a disservice to our students and the wider school community. We pray for fruitful dialogue within our school rather than a culture beset by moaning, grumbling and frustration. We ask too that any animosity or bitterness felt toward those in positions of authority would readily give way to collaboration and compassion. Thank you that, like your body, each member of staff plays an essential role in the day-to-day running of the school. Watch over our school's governance, we pray, keeping it in the defence of your watchful providence. May those who lead be used as instruments for your perfect will, that through their decisions you may be glorified.

We thank you that you are the true and worthy authority in our lives,

Amen.

Non-teaching Staff

Just as a body, though one, has many parts, but all its many parts
form one body, so it is with Christ. For we were all baptized by
one Spirit so as to form one body—whether Jews or Gentiles,
slave or free—and we were all given the one Spirit to
drink. Even so the body is not made up of one part but of many.

1 Corinthians 12:12-14

Gracious Father,

Thank you that you created us all with special talents and unique skills; each with a specific role and designated purpose. Help us to use the gracious gifts that you have bestowed upon us to both serve one another, and equip and edify the body of Christ. We praise you particularly for the tremendous work done by the non-teaching staff in our school, and thank you for their dedication, commitment and loyal service. We pray that they may flourish in their work and that students and teaching staff alike would recognise and appreciate their instrumental contribution to the daily life and running of the school. Thank you for the existing relationships that I have with colleagues across the school and please help me to reach out in humble and submissive love to members of staff with whom I currently have little interaction. Please foster a greater sense of collaboration between teaching and non-teaching staff, reflecting the fact that your church is composed of many members, with varying gifts and experience.

In your tender mercy and loving kindness we pray,

Amen.

Staff Morale

The thief comes only to steal and kill and destroy; I have come
that they may have life, and have it to the full.

John 10:10

Blessed Redeemer,

We find immense joy in living lives that glorify you, and through virtuous and godly living, point others to your saving death and the fullness of redemption. Thank you that teaching brings new insight and perspective on a daily basis. We know, however, that working in school can be tiring, stressful and frustrating. In these moments, we ask that your great peace and renewal would take root in our hearts. Redeem our frustrations, we pray, and help us to set any anxiety or self-pity firmly in the structure of your mighty acts of salvation, as wondrously revealed in Christ. Remind us also that the trappings of work are light and momentary when compared with the superior greatness of an eternity with you. We pray that we would be compassionate colleagues, looking out for those in trouble and accepting the help of others with humility and gratitude in our own times of need. Above all, we pray for unity among the staff in our school. Make us one in peace and the innumerable facets of your everlasting love, eager to serve one another with a willing mind and undivided heart.

Christ graciously hear us,

Amen.

Relationships of Grace

A new command I give you: Love one another. As I have loved you, so you must love one another. By this everyone will know that you are my disciples, if you love one another.

John 13:34-35

Our Teacher and Example,

Your command to love others the way you perfectly love us is easy to say but ever so hard to put into practice. All too often, we find ourselves quick to judge and condemn. I pray that, like you, I would be slow to anger and quick to love my colleagues, remembering that all are infinitely precious in your sight. Help me, Lord God, to channel my thoughts into how I can practically serve fellow staff members and give me words not of arrogance or criticism, but encouragement and compassion. Thank you that when we love others, we are manifesting the merciful and all-consuming love you showed us in your son. We also thank you that you never withhold good things from those who place their trust in your inexhaustible mercy, and ask that you would help us to demonstrate your perfect charity in our daily interaction with colleagues. May relationships of grace abound at my school, and may all come to abide in the safe shelter of your love.

We thank you for your steadfast love and abundant mercy,

Amen.

Professional Development

Praise be to the God and Father of our Lord Jesus Christ! In his great mercy he has given us new birth into a living hope through the resurrection of Jesus Christ from the dead, and into an inheritance that can never perish, spoil or fade. This inheritance is kept in heaven for you, who through faith are shielded by God's power until the coming of the salvation that is ready to be revealed in the last time.

1 Peter 1:3-5

Risen Lord,

May we experience the redeeming power of your resurrection at work in us. Help us to willingly seek opportunities to learn about pedagogy, share examples of good practice with colleagues, and engage in educational research. Purge our motives of all sin and self-congratulation, we pray, that we would be motivated to develop our teaching practice and quick to challenge ourselves professionally, not for the sake of career progression or good standing among fellow staff members, but to improve the quality of education that our students receive. Thank you for those who conduct valuable and rigorous educational research, may their work bear much fruit in the classroom. You are a God who teaches. May we, your children, be those who listen. Incline our ears to your perfect and inscrutable wisdom, that we might experience the heights and depths of the living hope to which you call us.

We ask these things in the name of our Lord and living Saviour, Jesus Christ,

Amen.

Work-life Balance

Come to me all who are weary and heavy-hearted, and I will give
you rest. Take my yoke upon you and learn from me, for I am
gentle and humble in heart, and you will find rest for your
souls. For my yoke is easy and my burden is light.

Matthew 11:28-30

Beautiful Saviour,

You created the world in six days and on the seventh day you sanctified a day of rest for all your creatures. I pray that amidst the hustle and bustle of the school term, I would set aside periods of rest, cherish time spent with loved ones, and devote myself to the regular study of your saving Word. Thank you that time itself belongs to you, and that you constantly enable me to meet deadlines and work with diligence and precision. On days when I feel frustrated and overwhelmed by my workload, remind me that you give safe lodging and secure haven to all who are weary and heavy-laden. Protect me, merciful God, from making an idol out of productivity and losing sight of the welfare and educational needs of the children placed under my care. I also ask that you would help me to be better at looking out for and supporting colleagues who feel stressed or overworked, encouraging them to place their burdens upon you. Grant me a heart of wisdom as I seek to balance my professional commitments with Church and family life, and most importantly help me to prioritise time spent in communion with you.

I rest my heart and hope in you,

Amen.

Health and well-being

The LORD is my strength and my shield; my heart trusts in him,
and he helps me. My heart leaps for joy, and with my song I
praise him.

Psalm 28:7

Comforter of the afflicted,

Every breath we take, every beat of our heart, is an extraordinary gift of unmerited grace, for which we praise and adore you. In times of ill-health would we be reminded of our Saviour's supreme act of self-sacrifice upon the cross, and hold fast to the security, strength and hope of his glorious resurrection. Thank you, God of justice, that you do not forget the cry of the needy and afflicted. Grant your loving protection to all in our school suffering in mind, body and spirit, both staff and students, and bring peace and consolation to those struggling with long term illness. We also ask that you would help us to be considerate, kind and attentive colleagues, sensitive to the well-being of fellow staff, and ready to actively listen and offer our services whenever the opportunity arises. Show us more of Jesus, we pray, that we may love as he faithfully loves us, and delight in the inexhaustible riches of his grace and compassion, in sickness and in health.

In the name of Jesus, the great physician,

Amen.

Chapter Three

For our School

For our School

Now I am about to go the way of all the earth. You know with all your heart and soul that not one of all the good promises the LORD your God gave you has failed. Every promise has been fulfilled; not one has failed.

Joshua 23:14

Radiant King of light,

Thank you for the provision of schools up and down the country, and for the particular school in which we work. Thank you for the students, staff and various resources that you have blessed us with. Would we be continually reminded of our utter helplessness without you, in all that we do, and forever grateful for your daily provision. You are a faithful God who keeps his promises, and through the peaks and troughs of our school's history, you have ensured that the doors stay open. We praise you for the learning that has taken place in our school in the past, and pray for the future education of the children entrusted to our care. We thank you too that every school is unique and pray that you would help us to protect and celebrate this diversity within our communities, that they might better reflect the radiance of your kingdom.

Bless and uphold our school, we pray,

Amen.

The Ethos of our School

Again he said, "What shall we say the kingdom of God is like, or what parable shall we use to describe it? It is like a mustard seed, which is the smallest of all seeds on earth. Yet when planted, it grows and becomes the largest of all garden plants, with such big branches that the birds can perch in its shade".

Mark 4:30-32

Glorious Lord,

Help us to view our school as a mustard seed, knowing that it is by your triumphant grace alone that it will flourish and grow into a place of beauty and hope. May the ethos of our school be one that celebrates and respects your creation, enriches and encourages the talents of our students, and seeks to serve the wider community. Whether the ethos is inherently Christian or not, may the leaders of our school seek to promote and develop Christian values amongst our students, teaching them to be kind, patient, forgiving and selfless. May the curriculum be designed in such a way that every aspect of your world is viewed as a lens for exploration and discovery. Keep our hearts open and minds inclined to you, we pray, as we plan and prepare to equip our students for the future.

In the name of Jesus our rock, fortress and salvation,

Amen.

Pastoral Care

I am the good shepherd. The good shepherd lays down his life for the sheep.

John 10:11

Saviour and mighty Deliverer,

Like sheep, we so often go astray, rejecting your promises and opting to live with spiritual self-sufficiency. With an unforgiving spirit, we crown ourselves in your place. Forgive us, merciful and loving Father, and put to death all that is self-exalting and arrogant in our lives, that we may, with a sincere willingness, turn away from sin. Thank you so much, our gracious Lord, that you are the Good Shepherd who draws near to us whenever we wander and never fails to lead us home. We pray that, as protectors of the children you have placed under our supervision, we would be continually reminded of how you shepherd us and reflect the unshakable hope that we have in you in our pastoral care of others. Help us to pursue justice when we monitor the playground, listen attentively when children share their problems with us, and enable reconciliation wherever possible. All-knowing Lord, in an ever-changing world where technology is used more than ever, show us as teachers ways to protect children and grant them your heavenly aid that they would make safe, responsible choices. Protect us, we pray, from spiritual pride and self-righteousness, and lead us in your way of real humility and patience, so that we may facilitate the integration of those who feel like lost sheep into our school community.

You are the Good Shepherd, Lord, and we surrender our lives to you,

Amen.

Finances

Do not store up for yourselves treasures on earth, where moths and vermin destroy, and where thieves break in and steal. But store up for yourselves treasures in heaven, where moths and vermin do not destroy, and where thieves do not break in and steal. For where your treasure is, there your heart will be also.

Matthew 6:19-21

Our Father in heaven,

In today's world, some schools feel more like businesses than places of learning. We pray that would not be the case. Instead, we ask that the quality of education our students receive and the passion and enthusiasm of their teachers would be of utmost importance to those leading our school. We pray that you would continue to provide for our school financially, that staff may not be made redundant, and that resources would be well looked after and replenished in a timely manner. In this vein, we pray that students would use equipment and resources with care and respect. We ask too that our government may see education as an essential and apposite investment, and that they will prioritise spending on education within their budget for the sake of current students and future generations. Help those who have authority over our school's budget to make wise, measured and godly decisions about how money is spent. Help us all to be radically generous with our money, setting a good example to those we teach, and reminding them that true wealth is only found in Christ. Grant that we, with joyful readiness, would give of ourselves and our material wealth in a sacrificial way.

Make us joyful givers like our Lord and Saviour, Jesus Christ,

Amen.

Resources

Because of the Lord's great love we are not consumed, for his compassions never fail. They are new every morning; great is your faithfulness. I say to myself, "The LORD is my portion; therefore I will wait for him".

Lamentations 3:22-24

Our giving God,

Thank you that your great spiritual blessings come afresh each morning, and that you are a faithful and loyal God who is worthy of our loving devotion and faithful worship. Thank you for the myriad provisions you afford us, especially those resources that facilitate our children's education. Thank you for the books that they read, the equipment they use, and the school buildings in which they feel safe and secure. You are a God who abundantly provides and sustains our schools. We pray that where gaps exist in our resources, we would patiently wait and seek constructive solutions. We pray too that we would treat our resources with respect and care, and encourage our students to do the same, that they may be used and enjoyed by generations to come. May we be generous in sharing resources with the schools around us and seek to raise funds for schools across the world who have much less than we do. We ask, gracious Father, that you would continue to pour out your blessings upon our school, that we may be faithful stewards of the resources you have given us.

Thank you for giving us yourself in Jesus Christ,

Amen.

Special Educational Needs

For you created my inmost being; you knit me together in my mother's womb. I praise you because I am fearfully and wonderfully made; your works are wonderful, I know that full well.

Psalm 139:13-14

Creator God,

Thank you that each of us is uniquely created in your image and likeness; with purpose and intricacy. I thank you for the students in my class who have particular learning difficulties or educational needs. Loving Father, would you help me to accommodate the particularities of their individual needs and differing temperaments that they might thrive under my care and reach their full potential. I pray both for students with physical impairments and for those with disabilities that we can't necessarily see, that you will make yourself known to them and that their hearts may be transformed by the living hope of the gospel, and the blessed promise of everlasting life. Help us to give them the support and resources that they need to flourish and grow at school. I pray that as a school we would be inclusive and compassionate towards all students, and that as teachers we would seek to unlock the potential of each student, in thankful and hallowed remembrance of your great goodness and perfect design for our lives.

Thank you that you bring steadfast and immovable hope to all,

Amen.

Links with other Schools

Speaking the truth in love, we will grow to become in every
respect the mature body of him who is the head, that is, Christ.
From him the whole body, joined and held together by every
supporting ligament, grows and builds itself up in love, as each
part does its work.

Ephesians 4:15-16

Sovereign King and Ruler of all nations,

Our school is one of several in the local area, one of thousands across our country, and one of millions across the world. Thank you that by virtue of our common task we are in partnership with educators across the world. We pray for education in our local area, that we would be at the forefront of sharing ideas and resources. Help us to foster strong links with schools of different ages, faiths and wealth, and cross national and linguistic borders, that we may extend the powerful hand of friendship to other schools and in so doing reflect the glorious riches of Christian fellowship. May we willingly support those schools where troubles pervade, and joyfully accept the help of others with true and sincere humility when we face our own trials. Give us the grace not to mark our success by the quality of examination results, but by the character and formation of our students. Let us not make rivalry and competition with other schools into an idol, but instead help us to cultivate a climate of collaboration within our communities.

Lord Jesus, hear our prayer,

Amen.

Presence in the Wider Community

Each of you should use whatever gift you have received to serve others, as faithful stewards of God's grace in its various forms. If anyone speaks, they should do so as one who speaks the very words of God. If anyone serves, they should do so with the strength God provides, so that in all things God may be praised through Jesus Christ. To him be the glory and the power for ever and ever. Amen.

1 Peter 4:10-11

Father of mercies,

Thank you for the community in which my school is located. Thank you for the different generations living together in one place and for the diversity that your mighty hand has brought into being. Give us as teachers a greater love for the community that surrounds us and help our school to be a source of energy, enthusiasm and generosity to all with whom we come into contact. All-powerful Lord, in every avenue of our lives, help us to look outwards for opportunities to serve others, rather than inwards in a bid to serve ourselves. Let us teach our children the importance of community projects and charity events, that they may grow into kind and selfless adults who view diversity not as something to fear, but something to celebrate. May those in the wider community feel welcome in our school, and willing to actively participate in the life of the school. Lord Jesus, bring your radiant light into our school that it may shine as a beacon of hope for the lost and broken in our communities.

Thank you that our school is part of a much bigger family,

Amen.

Chapter Four

For our Teaching

For our Teaching

Let my teaching fall like rain and my words descend like dew,
like showers on new grass, like abundant rain on tender plants.

Deuteronomy 32:2

Our teaching God,

Each day you use your living and active Word, your people, and the world that surrounds us to grant new wisdom and perspective to your children. Thank you that your teaching is as abundant as the falling rain. Grant us the energy and compassion to teach our students in a way that inspires and motivates them, just as you teach us. Equip us with the skills and knowledge to teach the whole gamut of academic and vocational subjects available at our school. Give us uncompromising courage to draw near to the liberty and joy of the gospel when our teaching feels ineffective and stale. Have mercy on us, loving Father, when our teaching inevitably falls short of your glory; and forgive us when we are quick to chastise and slow to nurture. May we share fully in the action and fruits of the Spirit, and be filled with gentleness and loving kindness that our students would freely come to us when facing difficulty and hardship. We also ask that you would help us to be fair and effective custodians of discipline in the classroom. Thank you for this great calling you have given us as teachers, let us take it up with full confidence that you walk alongside us in every moment of our day.

In the name of Jesus, our advocate,

Amen.

For Patience

My flesh and my heart may fail but God is the strength of my
heart and my portion forever.

Psalm 73:26

Lord of all,

Help us to rest in your calm strength and patient wisdom, and find peace and consolation in your promises, as we remember the endurance of your costly love for us; that while we were undeserving sinners, Christ died for us. Carry us, Father, that when we fall prey to the pangs of disillusionment and become frustrated by students' attitudes or by our growing workloads, we would know deeply that you alone sustain us. Help us to be patient with our words and our time, knowing that every second of our lives is a free gift from you. Let us be patient in the way we treat our students, by calling to mind your wonderful constancy and compassionate care. Thank you that each time we wander or lose our way, you, our Shepherd, patiently lead us home. In triumphant praise, we look to the perfect example of untiring patience exhibited in the life, death, and resurrection of Jesus.

Humble and contrite in spirit we pray,

Amen.

For Creativity

Yet you, LORD, are our Father.
We are the clay, you are the potter;
we are all the work of your hand.

Isaiah 64:8

Maker of heaven and earth,

How marvellous are the works of your mighty hand, our Creator and Redeemer. How beautiful and intricate is your loving design. Our work is your work, therefore reveal to us the unsearchable wealth of your creativity, we pray, and enable us to work in a way that is holy and acceptable to you, that your perfect son may be glorified through our labour. Whether we are designing a new curriculum or planning a lesson, marking a book or giving an explanation, infuse us, Father, with your insight, innovation and unclouded vision. Fill us with the ineffable joy of your salvation that we may find the time and energy to create. And help us to imbue that same sense of creativity in the children under our care, that they might be inspired to design, produce and imagine – in awe and wonder of their Father in heaven. Thank you for the splendour and glorious excellencies of your creation, and thank you for making us creative and bold creatures. Let us appreciate and marvel at your spectacular design, from the setting of the sun, to the laughter of a child.

Glory to you, O Father,

Amen.

For Resilience

Therefore, my dear brothers and sisters, stand firm. Let nothing move you. Always give yourselves fully to the work of the Lord, because you know that your labour in the Lord is not in vain.

1 Corinthians 15:58

Light of the world,

There are days when I find it difficult to go into school, days when the burden of work seems too great. Teach me, in your purifying and mighty power, to face challenges at work in the light of the gospel. Help me, Father, to place Jesus at the forefront of my mind when my heart is weary and heavy laden and storms seem unyielding. In trusting obedience would I turn my dissatisfactions over to you, gracious Lord, and seek your face and the security of your unfailing providence. Remind me that we do not preach ourselves, for how weak our case would be, but we boldly proclaim Christ crucified and risen. Therefore, we do not lose heart when our work is hard, our hours long and our students disobedient, for hope fortifies faith. Grant us, we pray, a deeper faith, courage and unity, that we may stand heavy-hearted but not crushed, and struck down but not destroyed. Your gospel, O Lord, is the antidote to all our troubles and all our weakness. May it shine ever more brightly today, for your glory.

You alone, Lord Jesus, can satisfy the deepest longings of my soul,

Amen.

For Discipline

For the Spirit God gave us does not make us timid, but gives us power, love and self-discipline.

2 Timothy 1:7

God of power, love and might,

Thank you for the ways you have disciplined and delivered your people, O Lord. May the way you instruct and discipline us serve as our model for discipline in the classroom. For because you are slow to anger and abounding in merciful love, we are able to present our bodies as a living sacrifice to you, and bring forth the fruits of holiness and righteousness. May I therefore, O God, stay calm and composed as I teach my lessons, be forgetful of past ill-will and treat my students with respect and compassion. Help me to recognise and celebrate the uniqueness of each child, and be fair and consistent in my management of the classroom. Through the proper ordering of my own life, which you alone see in secret, help me, loving and providing Father, to teach students respect through the way I conduct myself, that they will grow up to learn that embedded within the fabric of our own lives is the call to love our neighbours as ourselves. Flood my heart with grace when I am frustrated by students' behaviour and remind me of the true repentance and reconciliation that you so freely give us in your son. Lord Jesus, give me conviction in my instruction and deepen my goodwill toward my students and my love for you.

Thank you for your compassion and fatherly discipline,

Amen.

For Collaboration

Though one may be overpowered, two can defend themselves.
A cord of three strands is not quickly broken.

Ecclesiastes 4:12

King of Glory,

You are Father, Son and Holy Spirit, a trinity of everlasting love. We thank you that you are a relational God and that the need for human relationships is deeply imprinted in our hearts. Grant to us, our loving God, the gift of fruitful collaboration; both in our departments and school communities. Remind us that, as your chosen people, we are designed to collaborate and created to join together in our work. Thank you for those colleagues with whom working together comes naturally and grant us the humility and selflessness to serve alongside those with whom we naturally have a weaker affinity. Help us to stand against the idea that we are in competition with one another, and challenge hierarchical imbalances within the organisation of our school. Unite us in one purpose as children of one Father, that we would faithfully bear one another's burdens and joyfully seek one another's welfare. Root our desires in your will, we pray, and lead us to those who share a common need and express a shared devotion, that we might with one voice glorify your holy name.

For your great name's sake we pray,

Amen.

For Compassion

And the word of the LORD came again to Zechariah: "This is what the LORD Almighty said: 'Administer true justice; show mercy and compassion to one another'".

Zechariah 7:8-9

God of all compassion,

Your benevolence is higher than any mountain, deeper than any ocean and wider than the universe itself. We praise and honour you, our Father, that you gave up your one and only-begotten son, the radiance of your glory, that we could be washed clean. Thank you for your compassion and preserving grace. We pray as teachers that we would show great kindness to our students, understanding that they, like us, are fallible and will make mistakes. Grant us all a spirit of humility and conviction, and a firm desire for repentance and amendment, that we might forgive one another fully and freely, as you forgave us. Teach us to take into account and be sensitive to disparities in the home environment of our students. Just as we have been restored to a relationship with you through the precious blood of your dear son, help us to promote reconciliation and restoration in the classroom. Above all, Lord God, we pray that in showing compassion, we would display the character of Christ that our students might know more of your self-giving and unquenchable love.

Thank you that you are a God of unfailing love and everlasting consolation,

Amen.

For Inspiration

May the God of hope fill you with all joy and peace as you trust in him, so that you may overflow with hope by the power of the Holy Spirit.

Romans 15:13

Awe-inspiring God,

We need only a glimpse of an autumnal sunrise or the scent of the sea to know of the glorious majesty and splendour of your creation. The smallest breath of wind on our cheek reminds us of the intricacy and grandeur of all that you have made, and speaks to us of your greatness. In our classrooms and in our teaching, enlighten our understanding of you, we pray, that we might inspire the next generation to magnify your holy name. For yours is an everlasting light that will never fade. With exuberance and jubilation, every inch of creation sings of your unimaginably glorious and unending praises. Let us inspire the children under our care to join this majestic chorus of true devotion and thanksgiving, with a ready tongue for witness and praise. In each lesson that we teach, would you fill us anew with inspiration and creativity and bless each conversation we have that we would build up the children under our supervision. Help us too, we pray, to be wise role models for the children we teach, that they may learn more about you as they watch us. Thank you that you, the author of all life, never cease to inspire and amaze us.

In Jesus' pure and powerful name we pray,

Amen.

Chapter Five

For Education

For Education

Above all else, guard your heart,
for everything you do flows from it.

Proverbs 4:23

Our Strength and Preserver,

While educational policies, targets and priorities are susceptible to change of a seemingly constant nature, you, O Lord, remain the same. Your faithfulness to us does not waver; your blessings make our hearts sing each day. My lips are filled with your praise and benediction. For each morning, you give us 10,000 more reasons to give thanks. We pray for the future of education and the learning of generations to come. We ask, Lord, that you would give wisdom and discernment to those making decisions about education, from a local to an international level. We pray that they would seek to make "getting an education" a holistic and fulfilling experience, focused on much more than grades and examination results. May the education of today and tomorrow equip young people with skills for life, and foster within them a life-long love of learning and discovery. We also ask that teachers would be given sufficient time and space to nurture those most full of promise in their care. We thank you, Lord Jesus, for the great gift of education.

We pray that you would be honoured in our work as educators,

Amen.

Holistic Education

The LORD does not look at the things people look at. People look at the outward appearance, but the LORD looks at the heart.

1 Samuel 16:7

God of all consolation,

You do not look at our external accomplishments or outward acts, but you see us as spotless and perfect when we place our trust in your perfect son. Thank you, merciful Father, that you see beyond our flaws and imperfections. Thank you that you know us completely, and in spite of our bondage to sin, love us unconditionally, and lead us into life everlasting. We pray that the educational structures of today would mirror this liberating truth, and that it would inform our interaction with staff and students alike. We ask, loving Father, that you would give us observant eyes to look beyond the academic profile and success of our students and instead enable us to respect and care for them as your dearly loved children. We also pray that our schools would see the value of a holistic education, and recognise that the social, moral and spiritual development of students is just as important as their academic progress. Thank you, Lord, that you teach us to look beyond first appearances, with purity of affection may we centre our gaze on your wonderful deeds.

With a contrite and thankful heart we pray,

Amen.

Opportunities for All

There is neither Jew nor Gentile, neither slave nor free, nor is there male and female, for you are all one in Christ Jesus.

Galatians 3:28

Great God of peace,

Your gospel reaches all the nations and is a free gift available to all who call upon your name. We pray that such glorious gospel equality would be mirrored in our schools. Forgive us, Lord, for the way we prioritise certain groups of people with regard to access and quality of education, and help us to heal lines of division and foster the integration and inclusion of all. We pray that we would be those who champion the rights of every child to a free education, recalling the infinite mercies that you have afforded us as your adopted children. We also ask that across the world children would have the freedom to learn, develop and flourish in safe and supportive school environments and that you would bless those who teach them with impartiality and fairness. Grant, O Father, that the poorest in our communities would be provided with access to educational opportunities. We thank you that because of your saving death we are all your children, regardless of race, wealth, age or status, and we ask that the breadth and depth of this redeeming grace would fuel our desire for greater solidarity in every corner of your creation. We ask all of these things not with a view to exalting our own moral prowess, but for the glory of your beautiful son.

Penitent in spirit we pray,

Amen.

Technology

But Joseph said to them, "Don't be afraid. Am I in the place of God? You intended to harm me, but God intended it for good to accomplish what is now being done, the saving of many lives".

Genesis 50:19-20

Most high God,

Our classrooms look remarkably different to those of previous generations and we thank you for the great technological advancements that have been made. We particularly thank you for the efficacy of modern technology in our educational spaces. However, we are all too aware of the dangers that technology can pose. Let us not become lazy or disorganised in the face of new technology. Instead, O Lord, help us to look at how these new resources can best complement and enhance our teaching practice rather than detract from, and undermine, our interaction with students. Help us to cultivate social and communicative skills among our students, both with and without the use of technology, and grant us a deep wisdom as we seek to educate our children about the dangers of technology. Thank you that our students often display formidable proficiency and surpassing skill in their use of technology. Grant that we would be watchful for opportunities to learn from one another, and transmit our experience to those under our charge, with grace and humility. We also ask that technology would continue to be used in innovative and creative ways to improve the learning experiences of our students. However, we pray, O God, that these advancements would not distract or inhibit their educational development.

All glory and honour are yours,

Amen.

A Platform for Change

Now to him who is able to do immeasurably more than all we ask or imagine, according to his power that is at work within us, to him be glory in the church and in Christ Jesus throughout all generations, for ever and ever! Amen.

Ephesians 3:20-21

Redeemer of the World,

We know that education can serve as such a powerful tool for change, and yet we are also acutely aware that throughout history schools have been places of great discrimination, persecution and suffering. We ask therefore, our holy Father, that you would use Christian teachers across the world to promote and expound the multiple benefits of a strong and robust education. May we be quick to listen to the concerns of others, and slow to complain or act impulsively when our opinions differ from those around us. Loving Father, we humbly beseech you, that you would instil in us a due sense of purposeful responsibility that we might use our positions of authority to eschew the manward spirit of the age, and reflect the treasures of your wisdom. In this vein, we pray that the classes and educational programmes we offer would provide students with opportunities to excel, bringing skills, meaning and steadfast hope to broken communities and families. We also pray for the policy-makers in our country, and across the world, that they might promote fairness and equity of opportunity. May our classrooms and schools be powerful platforms for transformation and renewal.

How wonderful a vocation it is to serve you by educating the next generation,

Amen.

Future Educators

Jesus Christ is the same yesterday and today and forever.

Hebrews 13:8

Living Word,

Thank you that while the face of education is rapidly changing, and teacher recruitment, retention and morale seem to be in a state of perpetual decline, you remain the same. Your passion to teach future generations does not falter. Grant that educational policy and the training programmes of today and tomorrow would bring stability to our educational landscape and equip those entering the profession with the requisite skills to enthuse and inspire their students. May the educators of the future share your abiding love with the children under their care, and provide all-important moral instruction in the face of ever-changing educational contexts. We pray particularly for trainee teachers under our supervision that you would enable us to walk in meekness, charity and lowliness of spirit, as we teach them to teach, and help them to lay the necessary foundations for practical, faithful and steady service. We pray too that they would be well supported by the wider school and the programmes in which they train. Thank you for the generations of teachers to come, many of whom will be our students today. Please help us to set a good example for them, and thank you that in the face of change, your redeeming purposes and universal affection are resolute.

In your all-sustaining name we pray,

Amen.

JAMES AND KATIE HOWARD

Global horizons

Therefore go and make disciples of all nations, baptizing them in
the name of the Father and of the Son and of the Holy Spirit,
and teaching them to obey everything I have commanded you.
And surely I am with you always, to the very end of the age.

Matthew 28:19-20

King of Kings,

As those liberated in Christ, you call us to make disciples of all the nations. Grant that we would have a vision for your world-wide purpose, in whichever part of the world you have placed us. Give us grace, humility and a lively faith, we pray, in order that we might shine as lights for your gospel in our schools. We ask, our Father, that the education we provide would not be limited to the four walls of the classroom but would broaden our students' imaginations and horizons, as we teach them of the infinite wonders and rich diversity of your creation. Help us to infuse them with both genuine habits of gratitude for the education they receive, and an awareness that other children of their age may well face very different circumstances and challenges. We pray for existing links with schools abroad, and that you would enable new relationships to flourish. May children across borders, and who speak different languages, have the opportunity to interact with, and learn from, one another. Grant that we would be chartable in our giving, and seek opportunities to fundraise for schools less fortunate than our own. Thank you, Father, that your self-giving love and amazing gospel forges friendships that stretch the length and breadth of the planet.

Let everything that has breath praise and honour you,

Amen.

New challenges

He who was seated on the throne said, "I am making everything new!". Then he said, "Write this down, for these words are trustworthy and true".

Revelation 21:5

Lord of Grace,

In living the life we should have lived, and dying the death we should have died, our Lord and Saviour, Jesus Christ, the pioneer and perfecter of our faith, makes all things new. We praise you, Father, that day-by-day our hearts and minds are spiritually transformed, as we are crafted into your image and likeness and made holy by your Word and your Spirit. Thank you that because of Jesus we are born into this imperishable hope, and help us to live Christ-exalting lives worthy of this calling. As teachers, we pray that we would trust you absolutely with every aspect of our work, from planning to marking and disciplining to encouraging. Be with us in the new challenges that the teaching profession faces, especially in times of frustration, when its feels as though our students' education is vulnerable to compromise. Let us lay every burden on you, knowing that you will never leave or forsake us. Remind us, O Lord, that your sanctifying and healing grace is sufficient for us in every step we take, and help us to reflect this in our thoughts and actions, that our students may get a glimpse of you in us. Thank you for the wonderful vocation to which you have called us, and for the unquenchable fire of divine love that surrounds us.

We worship and adore you, Lord Jesus,

Amen.

Concluding Prayer

And this is my prayer: that your love may abound more and more in knowledge and depth of insight, so that you may be able to discern what is best and may be pure and blameless for the day of Christ, filled with the fruit of righteousness that comes through Jesus Christ - to the glory and praise of God.

Philippians 1:9-11

God of all Creation,

We commend ourselves and our undertakings to you. Thank you that you give us infinitely more than we could ever ask or imagine, and that your Word and your Spirit sustain and fortify us day-by-day. May our professional conduct bring glory and honour to your name, and would we be distinctive in the way that we care and support the students that you have placed before us. Remind us that your sovereign grace is sufficient in all that we do, and confirm our calling and election, we pray, that we might faithfully share the gospel of Christ with our colleagues. We pray that you would bless and uphold the school in which we work, and the children who attend it, and grant that we would ever cherish the precious gift of education.

Gracious Lord, accept all of these prayers, through Jesus Christ our Lord, to whom be glory, honour, power and dominion now and forevermore,

Amen.

ACKNOWLEDGMENTS

We would like to express our gratitude to our families, for their continued support, encouragement and insight during the composition of this book. In addition, we would like to express a special thank you to Dr and Mrs Jefferys for looking over the final manuscript.

INDEX

THE LUCAN
MISSION

Printed in Great Britain
by Amazon

25229379R00071